Babes in the Wood

A Pantomime

Verne Morgan

A Samuel French Acting Edition

FOUNDED 1830

SAMUELFRENCH-LONDON.CO.UK
SAMUELFRENCH.COM

Copyright © 1980 by Verne Morgan
All Rights Reserved

BABES IN THE WOOD is fully protected under the copyright laws of the British Commonwealth, including Canada, the United States of America, and all other countries of the Copyright Union. All rights, including professional and amateur stage productions, recitation, lecturing, public reading, motion picture, radio broadcasting, television and the rights of translation into foreign languages are strictly reserved.

ISBN 978-0-573-16414-9

www.samuelfrench-london.co.uk

www.samuelfrench.com

FOR AMATEUR PRODUCTION ENQUIRIES

UNITED KINGDOM AND WORLD
EXCLUDING NORTH AMERICA
plays@SamuelFrench-London.co.uk
020 7255 4302/01

Each title is subject to availability from Samuel French,
depending upon country of performance.

CAUTION: Professional and amateur producers are hereby warned that BABES IN THE WOOD is subject to a licensing fee. Publication of this play does not imply availability for performance. Both amateurs and professionals considering a production are strongly advised to apply to the appropriate agent before starting rehearsals, advertising, or booking a theatre. A licensing fee must be paid whether the title is presented for charity or gain and whether or not admission is charged.

The professional rights in this play are controlled by Samuel French Ltd, 52 Fitzroy Street, London, W1T 5JR.

No one shall make any changes in this title for the purpose of production. No part of this book may be reproduced, stored in a retrieval system, or transmitted in any form, by any means, now known or yet to be invented, including mechanical, electronic, photocopying, recording, videotaping, or otherwise, without the prior written permission of the publisher. No one shall upload this title, or part of this title, to any social media websites.

The right of Verne Morgan to be identified as author of this work has been asserted by him in accordance with Section 77 of the Copyright, Designs and Patents Act 1988

CHARACTERS

Baron Hardup
Robin Hood
Maid Marion
Coke, a Robber
Tizer, another Robber
Nurse Maxidrawers
Sheriff of Nottingham
Mark, the Boy Babe
Susan, the Girl Babe
Fairy
Will Scarlet
Village Girl
Much-the-Miller
Little John
Friar Tuck
Alan-a-Dale
Chorus of Villagers, etc.
Dancers

ACT I
    SCENE 1   The Baron's Garden
    SCENE 2   On the Way to the Woods
    SCENE 3   The Village School
    SCENE 4   On the Way to the Woods
    SCENE 5   The Nursery

ACT II
    SCENE 1   Sherwood Forest
    SCENE 2   On the Way to the Woods
    SCENE 3   The Baronial Hall

MUSICAL NUMBERS

ACT I

1	"THE BARON'S LOVELY GARDEN" (*To the melody of "English Country Garden"*)	Villagers, Dancers
2	BRIGHT MILITARY-TYPE SONG	Robin, Villagers, Dancers
3	TRIO	Coke, Tizer, Sheriff
4	COMEDY DUET	Nurse, Baron
5	SONG	Marion, Babes
6	PRODUCTION NUMBER	Robin, Marion, Villagers
7	COMEDY DUET	Coke, Tizer
8	DUET	Will Scarlet, Village Girl
9	"BOYS AND GIRLS"	Villagers
10	PRODUCTION NUMBER	Villagers, Dancers
11	DUET	Mark, Susan
12	SONG	Robin
13	SONG	Sheriff
14	LULLABY	Marion
15	DOLL DANCE	Dancers
16	SONG	Baron
17	PRODUCTION NUMBER	Full Company

ACT II

18	PRODUCTION NUMBER	Choristers, Dancers
19	BIRD BALLET	Fairy, Dancers
20	COMEDY DUET	Nurse, Sheriff
21	DUET	Robin, Marion
22	CHORUS SONG	Coke, Tizer, Nurse
23	STATELY NUMBER	Baron's Guests
24	BRIGHT PRODUCTION NUMBER	Robin, Marion, Guests
25	DANCERS' SPECIALITY	Dancers
26	MARCH DOWN	Full Company
27	FINALE CHORUS	Full Company

BABES IN THE WOOD

Scene 1

The Baron's Garden

This represents the resplendent grounds surrounding the Baronial Hall. There is an abundance of flowers and greenery, backed by a vivid blue sky. To one side is the entrance to the Baronial Hall

As the CURTAIN *rises we are in the middle of a garden party which the Baron is giving to the villagers in honour of his two young wards who are due to arrive. There is an air of gaiety as the Chorus, including Much-the-Miller, Little John, Friar Tuck and Alan-a-Dale, sing the opening number*

>Music 1. THE BARON'S LOVELY GARDEN
>(*To the melody of "English Country Garden"*)

First Phase   Come, everybody, sing and dance,
    In the Baron's lovely garden.
  Maidens and men in sweet romance,
    Their fond hearts not to harden.
  Everyone excited, everyone invited,
    All in the swirl of this joyous day,
  E'en the birds and the bees are
    Singing in the trees
  In the Baron's lovely garden.

Second Phase Soon the babes will be upon the scene,
    In this quaint old English garden.
  Uncle too will step upon the green,
    With loving care to guard them.
  Join in the frolic, everything symbolic,
    Fairies, and Wood Nymphs with mortals too,
  Everyone congregate and celebrate,
    In the Baron's lovely garden.

"The First Phase" is sung again, and without pause the Dancers enter to do a Morris Dance, the Choristers grouping up-stage to

watch. The music is repeated from the beginning and taken straight through, or as the choreographer desires. At the end of the dance the Choristers and Dancers fall back forming a V for the Baron's entrance

Much-the-Miller A big cheer for the Baron.
All Hooray!

The Baron enters from the house

Baron Your appreciation touches me to the quick. This fête, as you know, is being given in honour of my two young wards who arrive today.
Little John (*coming forward*) On behalf of us all, Baron, a big thank you!
Baron And are you all enjoying yourselves?
All Yes!
Baron And am I not the kindest Baron in the world?
All Yes, yes!
Baron (*suddenly very serious*) Remember that! If ever you hear an unkind word about me, or an unfair accusation, remember —you knew the Baron to be the kindest man in the world!
Friar Tuck (*coming forward*) Our sincere condolences sire on your recent bereavement.
Baron Alas! My brother's death is a great sorrow. However, the company of his two young children will compensate a great deal.
Friar Tuck They will be a great comfort to you, Baron.
Baron Yes, yes, I'm sure!

The Sheriff enters

Sheriff Excuse me, Baron Hardup.
Baron Why, Sheriff! What brings you here?
Sheriff I'm here to give you a warning, you and your guests.
Baron A warning? Of what pray?
Sheriff A desperate man, sir. Known by the name of Robin Hood.
All (*in a loud stage-whisper*) Robin Hood!
Sheriff He was last seen in this area. There is a reward for his capture.

Act I, Scene 1 3

Will Scarlet We all know Robin Hood. He's a *good* man.
Sheriff He's an outlaw—a thief!
Will He robs the rich to give to the poor.
Baron (*alarmed*) Robs the rich does he? He must be apprehended at once!
Sheriff There's a price on his head of one hundred pieces of gold.
All Ooooh!
Sheriff One hundred pieces for his capture dead or alive.
Baron (*obviously a little shattered*) Come, Sheriff, come into my house and accompany me with a glass of wine. Something must be done about this scoundrel at once. I have a small niece and nephew arriving today.

The Baron and Sheriff exit to the house, talking as they go

Alan-a-Dale Three cheers for Robin Hood!

The Choristers give three sharp cheers as the orchestra strikes up a few bars of bright music

Robin Hood enters

Robin Hail, folks! What's all the cheering about?
Alan You!
Robin Me?
Friar The Sheriff's offering a reward for your arrest.
Robin And that's why you're cheering?
All No!
Will Robin, it was silly to come here.
Robin But the Baron's giving a fête, open to all.
Will Watch out the Baron's fête doesn't turn out to be *your* fate!
Robin (*laughingly*) You little fatalist!

They all laugh

Have no fear. I know how to look after myself. There is much wickedness in this village. What I need is a gang of men to help me stamp it out.
John I'll be one of your loyal followers.
Robin And who are you?
John I'm Little John, and I'll follow where 'ere you go.
Much And so will I. I'm Much-the-Miller.

They all crowd round

Robin Your name?
Alan Alan-a-Dale.
Robin You?
Will Will Scarlet.
Robin And—er—you?
Friar Friar Tuck.
Robin You don't look like a friar.
Friar Alas, like you I have been made an outlaw. But deep down I am a good man, sire, believe me.
Robin I do believe you, but next time I see you be in your robes. No member of Robin Hood's gang need disguise himself. It's agreed then—we attack the rich to defend the poor?
All (*shouting with hands raised*) Yes! Hooray!
Robin Well done! That's our motto! And after all . . . (*He goes straightaway into the chorus of a song*)

Music 2. A BRIGHT MILITARY-TYPE SONG

Robin starts the number, the others join in. It develops into a big marching ensemble. If desired the dancers can enter and do a marching routine

All exit as the song ends. Coke and Tizer, the Robbers, enter

They enter to pizzicato music and leap on fairy-fashion, taking huge steps. Coke who is leading suddenly stops and Tizer cannons into him

Coke (*mysteriously*) Shoooosh!
Tizer Shoooosh!
Coke Shoooosh!
Tizer I *am* shooooshing!
Coke Remember who we are.
Tizer Who are we?
Coke We're a couple of robbers. (*He commences the big steps again*)
Tizer (*following*) Shooosh! You're being followed.
Coke Who by?
Tizer Me!
Coke Fool! (*He gives him a slap*) Look at you! Just look at you!

Act I, Scene 1

Tizer (*twirling round and round in an endeavour to look at himself*) I can't. I'm inside myself.
Coke What kind of a robber do you think you are?
Tizer (*pulling himself up proudly*) A very *good* robber.
Coke You *musn't* be a good robber! (*He gives him a slap*) You've got to be a *bad* robber. (*He gives him another slap*)
Tizer Why?
Coke Eh?
Tizer Why have I got to be a bad robber?
Coke Don't ask me. All robbers are bad. Aren't they, kids? (*He awaits audience reaction*) There you are.
Tizer (*to the audience*) I'm not a bad robber am I? (*He awaits the audience reaction*) There you are. I told you I was a goody.
Coke You're a baddy! Like me! Now shut up! I tell you what we'll do, kids, every time you see us we'll shout out, "Hi! Hi!" and you shout back, "Stop thief!" Will you do that? Right, let's have a little rehearsal. (*They plug the gag to get the idea going*) That's fine, now don't forget, will you? (*They use this as a running gag throughout*)

The Sheriff and the Baron enter from the house. They are chatting away quietly and the Sheriff has a large sheet of paper which he pins up on the downstage side of the house-piece, offering the reward for the capture of Robin Hood

Coke Look out! Quick, here's the Sheriff, dob your nut!
Tizer (*dashing over to the Sheriff and giving him a dig*) Hi, look out here's the Sheriff, dob yer nut!
Coke (*dragging Tizer quickly away*) Fathead! He *is* the Sheriff.
Tizer (*to the Sheriff, giving him a hearty smack on the back*) Sorry, pal!
Sheriff Isn't it time you two layabouts did something useful?
Tizer Like what?
Sheriff Like catching Robin Hood, for instance.
Coke Robin Hood? He's just an amateur.
Tizer Another honourable profession ruined.
Sheriff Honourable profession? Don't make me laugh! You're just a couple of petty thieves.
Tizer We may be thieves but we're *not* pretty! (*He does a sissy walk round the stage and pretends to ogle the Sheriff*)

Coke What's that you're pinning up there, then?
Sheriff The reward for Robin Hood's capture.
Tizer ⎫
Coke ⎭ Reward? (*Speaking together*)

They run past the Sheriff to read the notice

Sheriff One hundred pieces of gold.

The Baron joins the Sheriff and together they walk towards the opposite exit, apparently deep in conversation

Coke (*overcome*) One hundred nicker! We could retire on that.
Tizer Would that keep me in the style to which I've been accustomed?
Coke Do you know how much a hundred nicker is?
Tizer No, I've never pinched so many nickers. How much is it?
Coke How much is it?

The Sheriff exits

Tizer Yes, how much is it?
Coke It's a—well—it's a hell of a lot.

The Baron strolls over to the robbers in thoughtful mood

Baron So! You are a couple of robbers!
Coke Yes, guv'nor, professionals of course. Very experienced, solid and reliable.
Tizer Background murky, parenthood unknown.
Baron (*thoughtfully*) What sort of jobs do you do?
Coke Nothing too big nothing too small.
Tizer (*producing a large visiting card from somewhere down in his bosom*) Pass the gentleman our card.
Coke (*giving the card to the Baron*) Our card, guv'.
Baron (*reading*) "Coke and Tizer. *Haute Couture!* Office hours nine to ten?"
Tizer That's in the evening, of course.
Coke Yes, we don't get up till late afternoon.
Tizer And then we have to have our high tea.
Coke It's so high, sometimes it smells.
Baron I can well believe it.
Coke Our catalogue is on the other side.
Baron (*turning the card over and reading*) "Robberies done, throats slit, ear 'oles cut off"?

Act I, Scene 1

Coke That's right guv'. We work seven days a week, and we hold our "at homes" every other Sunday.
Tizer That's if we'd got a home but we haven't, so we hold 'em in somebody elses home.
Coke Yes, usually when they're asleep.
Tizer We never wake 'em up, just slit their throats.
Coke We're very professional.
Baron (*thoughtfully and deliberately*) So you do murders!
Coke (*after a short pause*) Eh?
Tizer Pardon? (*He hits the "P" so hard he spits*)
Baron (*wiping his eye*) I said, you do murders.
Coke Oh, no, no, no!
Tizer What ever gave you that idea?
Coke We wouldn't *stoop* to murder.
Baron (*exasperated*) But you slit throats.
Tizer Oh we may slit the odd throat, and we might cut off an ear 'ole as an encore—but we wouldn't stoop to murder.
Coke My friend did stoop once.
Tizer Yes, but somebody caught me bending.
Coke (*retrieving the visiting card*) Well, if you'll excuse us, guv', we'll be on our way.
Baron Just a minute, just a minute! (*He looks around making sure they are not overheard*) Tell me, how would you like to murder a couple of kids?
Coke (*after a slight pause*) How big are they?
Baron Oh, quite small. A boy and a girl.
Coke (*after another slight pause*) Would they fight?
Baron You're not afraid are you?
Coke Oh no! No, we're not *afraid*.
Tizer Not if they won't fight, we're not!
Coke How much?
Baron Two hundred pieces of gold.
Coke (*to Tizer*) Two hundred nicker.
Tizer What for?
Coke To murder a couple of small kids.
Tizer Is that more than we get for Robin Hood?
Coke I'll ask him. (*To the Baron*) As a man of business, how does your offer compare with the Sheriff's?
Baron It's twice as much.

Coke (*to Tizer*) Twice as much.
Tizer So it should be, there's two of 'em. It'll take twice as long.
Coke Yes, we've got to think of the time. Well, what do you think?
Tizer Aye, we'll do it.
Coke (*to the Baron*) My partner's agreeable. When do we start?
Baron (*dropping his voice*) As soon as possible. Listen, I'll lure them out of the house and send them into the woods on some pretext. While they're at their play I'll slink off—and it's all yours.
Tizer *What's* he going to do?
Coke He's going to send the kids into the woods on a protest.
Tizer Ah well, that's very fashionable nowadays. I agree.
Baron Very well. I'll see you tonight!
Coke (*with dramatic gesture*) Tonight!
Tizer (*also with dramatic gesture*) Tonight!

Music 3 TRIO

(*Preferably a song in which they can over-dramatize the situation*)
The three of them sing with malicious intent. If possible the song finishes with a cod-dramatic dance

Coke, Tizer and the Baron exit at the end of the song. From the opposite side Nurse enters with the Babes, Mark and Susan. The Babes carry luggage. Nurse is full of bustle and hustle, talking and gesticulating at great speed

Nurse Here we are then, here we are! This is the house, not that way, over there, stupid. Put the luggage on the steps and ring the bell. We'll stand back so that Uncle can see us from a distance. We look better at a distance. *Put it on the steps!*

Mark
Susan } Yes, Nurse! } (*Speaking together*)

Mark and Susan make for the steps

Nurse Come back here!

They return to her quickly

Mark, put your hat on straight. (*She straightens Mark's hat, then gives him a little slap and a push towards the house*) Now put the luggage on the doorstep.

Act I, Scene 1

They start to go

Come back here!

They return quickly to her

Susan, pull your frock down. You're getting a big girl now. (*She adjusts Susan's frock*) Now hurry up and put the luggage on the doorstep. Hurry, hurry, don't dawdle! Come back here! Have you washed behind your ears? You sure? Well, go on, get rid of the luggage, what are you waiting for?

They dump the luggage and run back to Nurse

You didn't ring the bell!

They run to the house, pull the bell, then race back to her side. They stand in a line, half-facing the doorway in a pose ready to meet the Baron

Remember, you're going to meet your new uncle. He's never seen you before. Try to make a good impression. Stand nicely, and look happy. Go on, smile! *Smile!*

The Babes try to smile, but not very successfully

Like this. (*She puts her two forefingers either side of her mouth and stretches it into an enormous smile*)

The Babes look at her, then face the audience and do likewise

Oh my gawd! Look natural!

The Baron enters, and nearly measures his length over the luggage. He gathers himself and gives the luggage a hefty kick, injuring his toe in the process

Baron Hardnut, I presume!
Baron (*coming forward*) And you—and you are my two lovely wards. Come and give your uncle a nice big kiss.
Mark I don't *kiss* people, I'm a boy.
Baron Oh, are you?
Mark Shake! (*He offers his hand*)

The Baron shakes it feebly

Baron And you of course are Susan. You're a girl so *you* can kiss me. (*He moves towards her*)
Susan (*backing away*) No! No!
Nurse She doesn't kiss strange men, she reckons it's unhealthy.
Baron But I'm your uncle—you can kiss *me*.
Susan (*hiding behind Nurse*) I'd rather not, if you don't mind.

The Baron thrusts his face forward. Nurse grabs it and kisses him passionately. The Babes go and pick up the luggage

Nurse There you are, now you've had it.
Baron (*recovering himself*) Good grief! (*He turns to the children who are awaiting instructions*) Take the luggage up to your bedroom, you'll find it on the first floor.

Mark and Susan exit

(*Rubbing his chin and watching the children depart*) Hmmm! Two hard little nuts!

Nurse Then you'll be three Hardnuts together! (*She laughs immoderately at her own joke till she sees the Baron's straight face*)
Baron (*acidly*) So you are the nurse! Hmm! What is your name?
Nurse (*brightly*) Nurse Maxidraws.
Baron (*aghast*)) Maxidraws? Heavens, haven't you another name?
Nurse Minnie.
Baron Minnie!
Nurse Yes, Minnie Maxidraws.
Baron (*distastefully*) I shall just call you plain nurse.
Nurse Don't emphasize the plain bit.
Baron (*aside*) I'd better butter the old girl up I suppose, it'll help my plan. (*To Nurse*) Tell me, Miss—er—Minidraws . . .
Nurse *Maxidraws!*
Baron Sorry! Maxidraws.
Nurse Don't belittle me, please!
Baron Do you care for the odd drink?
Nurse Not if it's too odd.
Baron Yes, I see what you mean. You prefer evens?
Nurse Two at a time.

Act I, Scene 1   11

Baron Then what about a couple of pints at the local.
Nurse What about the Babes?
Baron I've engaged a couple of men to look after them.
Nurse How many men have you engaged to look after me? (*She gives him a playful slap on the back which nearly knocks him for six*)
Baron You—you saucy besom! (*To the audience as he tenderly rubs his shoulder*) For crying out loud!

Music 4. COMEDY DUET

(*This should be a love duet, followed if possible with a burlesque dance*)

At the end of the song the Baron and Nurse exit arm in arm. The Babes enter from the house, holding hands. They have now taken off their hats and coats

Susan I don't think I'm going to like it here, Mark.
Mark Oh, we'll get used to it, I suppose.
Susan Oh, Mark! I don't know why, but I'm afraid.
Mark Don't worry, Susan, there's nothing to be afraid of. Come on.
Susan Where are we going?
Mark To the woods, those two men told us to go there.
Susan What for?
Mark To meet Uncle, they said he was waiting for us.
Susan I don't like those two men, they're silly.
Mark They said they work for Uncle, and we have to do what Uncle says.
Susan Oh very well, then. Come on.

Mark and Susan move to exit R

The Fairy enters up R, *and waves her wand*

The Babes do not see her. To them she is invisible

Mark (*stopping suddenly*) I don't know why, but something tells me not to go that way.
Susan Oh, Mark, how strange! I've got the same feeling.

They stroll back thoughtfully

Mark I suppose we're being very silly.
Susan Yes, and Nurse will be so cross if we disobey.
Mark Come on!

They again walk to exit R, and again the Fairy waves her wand as she smiles at them

No! I'm not going, and neither are you. Come on, my mind's made up. We'll go back to the house.

Maid Marion enters from the house. The Fairy exits R

Marion Hallo!
Mark⎫
Susan⎬ Hallo! ⎱(*Speaking together*)
Marion You must be the Baron's niece and nephew.
Mark That's right. I'm Mark and she's Susan. Who are you?
Marion I'm Maid Marion. I work for the Baron.
Susan As a maid?
Marion Yes!
Susan Oh good! I don't feel so miserable now.
Marion Miserable? You mustn't be miserable.
Mark (*putting his arm round Susan*) Well, you know, a little bit homesick.
Marion I know just how you feel.

Music 5. MARION'S SONG

(*She sings the number to the two Babes, and if wished they can join in*)

Marion, Mark and Susan exit at the end of the song. Nurse enters. At the same time, unseen by Nurse, the Fairy enters upstage and watches from a distance

Nurse (*who is very jolly*) Oh I say, what a nice man that uncle is He wanted me to go into the woods. He thought because I've had a couple I'd be easy. (*She laughs uproariously*) He doesn't know *my* capacity. "Get thee behind me, Satan," I says. So he got behind me and pushed me back into the pub. Now then, I wonder where those two Babes have got to?
Fairy If you hadn't gone off drinking with their wicked uncle you would know!

Nurse (*completely flummoxed, being unable to see the Fairy, who is invisible*) That's funny! Someone spoke but there's no one there.
Fairy Perhaps it's your guilty conscience pricking you.
Nurse Perhaps, if I had a conscience.

The Fairy walks down and positions herself immediately behind Nurse

Fairy (*speaking very deliberately*) Don't—trust—Uncle!
Nurse Extraordinary! I could have sworn someone said right into my shell-like earhole, "Don't trust Uncle."
Fairy Uncle has evil designs.
Nurse I knew it, I knew it! That man fancied me from the start.
Fairy Not on *you*! On the Babes.
Nurse I *have* got a conscience, and it's doing overtime. There are thoughts going through my head and I'm not putting them there.
Fairy It is me who is putting them there.
Nurse (*turning this way and that*) You? Who are you? Where are you? I can't see you!
Fairy You can't see me because I'm invisible. I'm a Fairy.
Nurse A Fairy!
Fairy Yes. I'm standing right behind you.
Nurse (*tiptoeing down towards the audience*) Can *you* see her? . . . Where is she, over here? . . . Over here . . . ? Over there . . . ?

The Fairy exits

Where is she now? . . . Gone? Gone where? . . . Aah! You're having me on. Yes you are. (*She drops her voice to a stage-whisper*) *Was* there a Fairy, honest? . . . Ooh! I'm going into the house to sober up.

Nurse exits. The Sheriff enters, pins up another, larger notice for the capture of Robin Hood, and exits. Robin Hood and his Men enter, go to the notice-board, read the poster, and laugh. Marion enters with several Choristers: they join Robin's men at the notice-board. There is murmuring as they read the notice

Robin is struck by Marion's beauty and just stands gazing at her

Robin Do you hope they catch him?

Marion Yes, I do.
Robin Don't you like outlaws?
Marion I don't like wicked men.
Robin How do you know he *is* wicked?
Marion I don't. I've never met him. Do you know him?
Robin I thought I did, but I'm beginning to wonder. (*He takes a step towards her*)

Music 6.
LARGE-SCALE PRODUCTION NUMBER

Scene 2

On the Way to the Woods

A leafy front-cloth scene

Coke and Tizer enter, followed by the Baron. The Robbers do their running gag

Baron (*who is very annoyed*) When are you going to get a move on? Those kids have been here a whole day and you haven't done a thing.
Coke We told 'em you were waiting for 'em in the woods but they came back.
Baron (*mimicking*) *They came back!* You should have gone with them.
Coke Ah, but you see we were minding your house.
Tizer Yes, we didn't like leaving the house unguarded with that chap Robin Redbreast lurking about.
Coke Robin *Hood*! (*He stamps on Tizer's toe*)
Baron You mean you didn't like leaving the house all the while there was a drop of wine left in the bottle.
Coke (*hurt*) I think that's very uncalled for!
Tizer So do I. Don't let's talk to him.
Baron I've got an idea.
Coke We're not talking to you.
Baron Listen to me. I've got an idea.
Tizer Sew a button on it.

Act I, Scene 2   15

Coke We're not talking to you.
Baron Nurse is opening a school so that the Babes can continue their education. I want you to disguise yourselves as a couple of small boys and go there.
Coke (*aghast*) What, go to school?
Baron Yes.
Coke⎫
Tizer⎭ We're not talking to you. ⎫(*Speaking together*)
Baron It won't do you any harm. You're both illiterate.
Tizer (*aside to Coke*) What does he mean by that?
Coke We haven't been circumvented.
Baron Yes, and I'll put on a disguise too, and meet you there—in the school.
Coke In the school?
Baron Yes. When schooltime is over we'll follow the Babes out, entice them into the woods, and then you can kill 'em.
Tizer Why do we have to kill 'em?
Baron That's what you're being paid for.
Tizer Can't we just give 'em a good hiding and send 'em home?
Coke Shut up! Remember, we're not talking to him.
Tizer Oh sorry, I forgot. We're not talking to you.

They both turn their backs on the Baron

Baron Listen, you two, listen to what I have to offer.
Tizer It's no use asking us to have a drink, we're not talking to you.
Baron I'll let you into a secret, never breath it to a soul. These two Babes have *got* to die. When their father died he left them his entire fortune, including the Baronial Hall in which I live. Should they die I inherit all the money. Get it?
Coke We're not talking to you.
Baron And the Baronial Hall reverts to me!
Tizer We're not talking to you.
Baron And you get two hundred golden nicker.
Coke⎫
Tizer⎭ *Now* we're talking to you. ⎫(*Speaking together*)
Baron Right! In the meantime keep a low profile. We'll meet in the schoolroom—disguised!
Coke You'll never disguise your ugly chops.

Baron Oh yes I will, I've thought up something special. (*He begins to laugh at his own thoughts*) Something very special. Ta-ta, see you in school, little boys.

The Baron exits, laughing heartily

Coke (*mimicking him*) Ha, ha, ha! And remember, he who laughs least loafs longest.

Music 7. COMEDY DUET—COKE AND TIZER

(*Preferably a number with audience participation*)

Coke and Tizer exit after their number. The Sheriff enters

Sheriff There's something strange going on round here and I don't like the smell of it. I distinctly overheard the Baron say something about attending the village school in disguise. Hmm! I think I'll keep an eye on those three.

The Sheriff exits. Will Scarlet and a Village Girl enter, skipping on, laughing and talking

Will Isn't it exciting? Nurse is opening a school and we're all invited.
Village Girl I've never been to school before.
Will Nor I.
Village Girl I wonder what it's like?
Will Like falling in love, I suppose.
Village Girl Then it must be wonderful.

Music 8.

DUET—WILL SCARLET AND VILLAGE GIRL

(*Preferably a modern number which can finish with a dance*)

Scene 3

The Village School

The teacher's desk in in the centre, a blackboard to one side. A cane lies diagonally across the desk. Long forms are placed "V" shape to accommodate the pupils

Act I, Scene 3

As the CURTAIN *rises, the Choristers, Dancers, and anyone else the producer wishes to include, are dancing and singing in small groups holding hands*

Music 9. BOYS AND GIRLS

All Boys and girls come out to play,
Hi-dee-diddle-dee-dighty-day.
Boys and girls come out to play,
Today is a holiday.

The singing is interrupted by Nurse (now called the Teacher) who enters ringing a large handbell. She careers round the stage, making a lot of noise

The pupils go to their places but remain standing

Teacher (*positioning herself behind the desk, and awaiting complete silence*) Scholars! Squat!

She makes an appropriate movement with her hands and they all sit to rhythm

First lesson today is singing.

Music 10. PRODUCTION NUMBER

(*The introduction strikes up immediately. This should be a bright applicable number and should preferably include the dancers*)

At the end of the number all sit

Teacher Now then, this morning we have two new pupils joining us. Who are they?

Mark and Susan skip happily on, holding hands

Mark
Susan } Here we are! } (*Speaking together*)

Teacher Ah! Mark and Susan. Say "Good morning" to your fellow pupils.

Mark } (*with a little movement of the hand*) Howdey } (*Speaking
Susan }   pupils!   }   together*)

All (*rising and also making a small movement with the hand*)
Howdey, Mark and Susan!

Teacher Yes, well, it's a permissive age I s'pose. Now, you two sit over there.

The Babes retire to a quiet spot L

Coke enters. He is dressed as a little boy, school cap, shorts, etc.

He struts straight up to the desk

Hallo, another new boy! What's your name?
Coke Willie Winklepop.
Teacher You're late.
Coke I had to go to the labour exchange to sign on for my father.
Teacher Why can't your father sign on for himself?
Coke He's working.
Teacher Sit over there.

She directs Coke to a form down R

Tizer enters. He also is dressed as a little boy. He walks through the door, knocks on it from the inside, then exits again

Come in. (*She looks up and sees no-one is there*) Funny! I could have sworn I heard a knock.

Tizer enters again and repeats the business, making a smart exit as before

Come in! (*She again looks up too late to see Tizer*) I must have bats in my belfrey!

Tizer enters again

This time Teacher watches him and waylays him as he is about to exit

What's the idea? Coming in here, knocking on the door, and then walking out again?
Tizer I didn't want to go to school.
Teacher So?
Tizer So I came inside to lock myself out.
Teacher What's your name?
Tizer I haven't got a name.
Teacher What do your friends call you?

Act I, Scene 3   19

Tizer Stinky.
Teacher Can you touch your toes, Stinky?
Tizer Oh yes, easy.
Teacher Bet you can't.
Tizer Bet I can.
Teacher Go on then. Lower—lower—right down. (*She whips the cane off the desk and gives him a slap across his posterior*)

Tizer hollars

   Clever boy! Now go and sit over there.

Still rubbing his hindquarters, Tizer takes a seat next to Coke

   The Baron enters. He is dressed as a little girl, short frock, long hair and much beribboned. He minces over to the teacher with studied elaboration

   What a pretty little girl! What's your name?
Baron Ermintrude.
Teacher I shall call you Ermine and leave the rude bit out.
Baron And look, Teacher, I've brought you a present. (*From somewhere deep down in his bosom he brings up an empty beer bottle from which protrudes a red rose*)
Teacher (*going into ecstasies*) Oh, how ecstatical! A rose by any other name! I shall treasure it always.
Baron Yes, I was tickled pink with it. (*He rubs his chest vigorously*)
Teacher (*placing the bottle-cum-vase on the desk*) Sit over there, rude Ermine.

The Baron dances gaily down to Coke and Tizer, seating himself between them. They put arms round each other and sway forward and backward, the movement getting larger and larger, till eventually they fall backwards on to the floor

   Who did that?
All Willie Winklepop!
Teacher Come out here, Willie Winklepop!

Coke is brought forward, protesting. Teacher removes his cap from his head and throws it on the floor

   Pick your rat up!

Coke bends to pick up his cap and she gives him a slap with the cane

(*Returning to the desk*) First lesson this morning is history.

Who was the Black Prince?
Tizer The son of Old King Cole.

Everyone laughs

Teacher Who said that?
All Willie Winklepop!
Teacher Come out here, Willie Winklepop!

Coke comes forward, protesting. Teacher removes his cap and throws it on the floor

Pick your rat up!

Coke bends to pick up his cap and gets another slap with the cane

Coke I never said a word.

Teacher returns to the desk and is interrupted by the Baron jumping madly up and down

Teacher What's the matter with you rude Ermine? Have you got Saint Vitus-is-is-isses dance?

The Baron hurries to Teacher and whispers something in her ear

Oh all right, hurry up then.

The Baron exits

Now then! What do we get from India?
Tizer India-rubber!

Everyone laughs

Teacher Who said that?
All Willie Winklepop!
Teacher Come out here Willie Winklepop! (*She removes his cap and throws it on the floor*) Pick your rat up!

Act I, Scene 3   21

The same business is repeated, Coke protesting vainly as he receives the cane

    Now sit down and behave.
Coke I'll behave, but I can't sit down.
Teacher (*shouting at him*) You're a Ninnie! You know what a Ninnie is?
Tizer A Nannygoat's sweetheart.

Everyone laughs

Teacher Who said that?

There is complete silence. Then Coke rises, walks to the middle of the room, throws his cap on the floor and bends down

Tizer (*as Teacher is about to hit Coke*) Stop! Stop! I cannot be such a cad as to let my friend suffer punishment for a crime of which I am guilty. It was I, I who said a ninnygoat was a nannygoat, and it is I, I who will take my punishment like a man.

Coke remains in the bending position. Tizer walks dramatically towards him, places his hands on Coke's waist and bends down behind him. As Teacher raises her cane, Tizer leapfrogs on to Coke's back, so that Coke receives the blow

Coke (*as they return to their places*) I must be using the wrong aftershave.

    The Baron enters and bounces boldly to his seat, passing Teacher on her way back to the desk

Teacher Well, rude Ermine, did you enjoy your glass of water.
Baron Yes, thank you.

Teacher (*looking at the audience*) See!

Tizer begins to blow up a large balloon. At first Teacher does not notice and goes on ad-libbing about the next lesson-to-be. The whole class begin to take huge in-and-out breaths in unison with Tizer as the balloon gets bigger and bigger. Teacher tiptoes towards him and, fascinated beyond all measure, joins in with the huge breathing. By now all are on their feet and gathered round Tizer suiting a large forward and backward movement with the body as they "blow". The balloon bursts. Everyone reacts, Teacher falling flat on her back. She gropes her way back to her desk and revives herself by frantically smelling the rose in the beer bottle. She then removes the rose and takes an imaginary swig at the bottle, following up with much hiccuping. Tizer calls her attention to something on the floor

Tizer Look Teacher, down there!
Teacher (*pulling herself together*) Where?
Tizer Down there! Look, thousands of 'em!
Teacher I can't see anything. (*She bends very low*) Where?

Tizer snatches the cane from her hand and gives her a clout across her bottom

Tizer There!

Tizer drops the cane and runs for his life. Teacher picks up the cane and chases after him. They weave in and out the forms. All the pupils are on their feet shouting encouragement to Tizer. They jump up and down and make a great deal of noise

When the chase has gone far enough Tizer exits, pursued hotly by Teacher. All make for nearest exits still shouting and laughing, with the exception of Mark and Susan

Mark and Susan come quietly downstage as the introduction to their number strikes up

Music 11. DUET—MARK AND SUSAN

SCENE 4

On the Way to the Woods

Robin enters, followed by Marion

Marion And still you won't tell me who you are?
Robin I'd like to keep it a secret—just a little longer.

Marion exits a trifle petulantly

Act I, Scene 4   23

Music 12. SONG—ROBIN

Robin exits after his number. Coke and Tizer enter, followed by the Baron. They are still in their school disguises

Baron You fools! You've missed 'em. They'll be home by now.
Coke We couldn't help it.
Tizer No, Teacher kept us in after school.
Baron And who's fault was that?
Tizer Teacher's.
Baron Teacher's?
Tizer Yes. She kep' on looking at me and saying I'd like to keep you in after school. I think she fancied me.
Baron (*hotly*) She kept you in after school because you're such a dunce!
Coke She kept you in too.
Baron That's beside the point. What matters is, we've got to lure those two kids into the woods and kill 'em.
Coke Can we have a bit on account?
Baron You'll get the money when the job is done.
Coke Suppose you don't pay up?
Baron In that case you can keep the Babes.
Coke That's no use to us, what are we going to do with a couple of dead kids?
Baron You can hang 'em on your watch-chain.
Tizer Who's going to pay the VAT?
Baron They're not registered. Now look, we're wasting valuable time. I tell you what, come to the Baronial Hall tonight. I'll leave a window open so you can break in. The Babes will be asleep in the nursery, you creep in quietly and abduct 'em. Right?
Coke Right!
Tizer Mind somebody doesn't abduct *you* in that glamorous get-up!
Coke Yes, beware you don't get chased up an ally by a sailor!
Baron (*cross and self-conscious*) Belt up! Stop talking drivel and follow me.

As they make for the exit Tizer lifts the Baron's skirt from behind and has a peep underneath

Coke, Tizer and the Baron exit. The Sheriff enters; he follows the retreating figures with a dubious eye, and rubs his chin thoughtfully

Sheriff Very strange goings on, very strange indeed.

Music 13. SONG—SHERIFF

SCENE 5

The Nursery

It is a typical child's nursery with a double bed in the middle of the room

As the CURTAIN *rises, the Babes are in bed and Marion is singing them a lullaby. Susan is dressed in a period nightgown and Mark in pyjamas*

Music 14. LULLABY—MARION

Marion (*after the singing*) Now come along, it's past your bedtime.
Mark Oh Marion, I don't want to go to bed.
Marion But you must go to bed. That's what beds are for, to go to.
Susan Can I have something to eat first?
Marion No you can't. Those who ask don't get.
Susan Well, can I have an apple if I don't ask for one?
Marion (*walking round the bed tucking them in*) Nurse will be along any minute, I don't know what she'll say if she finds you still awake.
Susan Nurse is a silly old woman.
Marion You musn't say that.
Susan But she is.
Mark She can't tell Coke from Pepsi.
Marion That's enough, you musn't criticize your elders.
Susan Marion! Is it true the stork brings babies?
Marion So they say, dear.

Act I, Scene 5   25

Mark I reckon the stork who brought Uncle must have been a vulture!

Marion You are not to talk about your Uncle like that. He has been very kind to you, taking you in after your father died, and caring for you, and everything.

Mark I don't know why, but there are two things in this world that I hate and he's both of them.

Susan Me too! I hate him, I hate him, I hate him!

Mark Three hates are twenty-four!

The Babes laugh at the joke, and after a moment Marion laughs too

Marion You will get to like him, I know you will. Now come along, off to bye-byes.

Marion sings a short reprise of the Lullaby as she exits

The Babes snuggle down. The Lights dim

The Fairy enters, walks over to the bed and waves her wand over the sleeping Babes

Fairy Sleep on, dear Babes, in peaceful bliss,
No harm shall ere befall you,
Just dream of toys you wish you had,
Their antics to enthrall you.

Music 15. DOLL DANCE

The Dancers enter and dance in stiff jerks as though made of wood. Any suitable music can be used

Mark and Susan sit up and watch the Dolls in wondrous delight. If wished, the choreographer can bring them into the dance

At the end of the dance, all exit, including the Babes. Nurse enters. She carries a lighted candle which she places on a small table by the side of the bed

Nurse Ah me! It's been a tiring day, I think I'll turn in with the Babes and have a spot of shut-eye. Would you mind turning your backs while I undress. (*She turns her back on the audience and begins to disrobe. She suddenly turns front and glares at the audience*). (*Shouting*) I said, "Turn your backs!" Really!

Such confustication I never before did see. (*She bellows*) *TURN YOUR BACKS!*

Nurse begins to disrobe again, occasionally regarding the audience with a baleful eye. The business can be arranged at the producer's discretion. There is soft music all through. She then brings forth a long old-fashioned nightgown from under the pillow and drapes herself in it. After which she hops into bed. She is about to blow out the candle when she remembers something. She gets out of the bed and looks underneath it. She pulls out a round white-coloured hat-box and from it withdraws an old-time mob-cap. She places it on her head and hops back into bed. Once again she prepares a big breath to blow out the candle, and once again she pauses. She gets out of bed and kneels by the side of it, hands together in supplication. The music stops

Oh, heavens above! Hear my plea if you can,
Get busy up there and send me a man! Aaah-men! (*She then gets back to bed, calls out "Goodnight" to the audience, and blows the candle out*)

The Lights dim

Coke and Tizer enter. They are now in their normal attire. Tizer is carrying a huge tool bag which he drops with a clatter as they enter

Coke Shut up! Don't·make a noise. The Babes are asleep.

Tizer trips over his feet and drops the bag again

Shooosh! Why can't you make a noise quietly.

They tiptoe to the bed and gaze at the bundle lying there

Tizer Is that 'em?
Coke Yes. People look different in bed.
Tizer You can say that again. Oh dear!
Coke What's the matter?
Tizer I want to sneeze.
Coke Well don't do it here, you'll wake 'em. Go in the corner and do it.

Tizer hurries on tiptoe to the corner downstage, makes a tremendous preparation, then gives an effeminate little sneeze. He hurries back to the bed. In the meantime Nurse turns over on to her stomach and raises her posterior well up under the bedclothes. The two Robbers stand gazing at the lump

Tizer Pardon me, is that a boy babe or a girl babe?
Coke I don't know, looks more like a rhinoceros suffering with the botts.
Tizer More bot than rhino!
Coke Yes. Tell you what, you take this one and I'll have the little'n.
Tizer I can't manage this one on my own, you'll have to give me a hand.
Coke Okay. Grab hold.

They struggle to lift Nurse up and, still covered with the bedsheet, they carry her shoulder-high and place her full-length on the floor

Tizer I reckon they got this babe in the Outsize Department.

As they stand puffing and blowing the Nurse wakes up. She throws the bedsheet off and sits up. She gives a delighted scream when she sees the men and jumps up

Nurse Aaah! A man, a man! My prayer has been answered!

She chases the Robbers round the stage, shouting, "A man, a man!" The Robbers, frightened out of their lives, run round the bed, over the bed, etc., shouting, "Help! Murder! Thief!" with the Nurse in hot pursuit

Coke, Tizer and Nurse exit in quick succession. The Baron enters from the opposite side, now in normal attire

Baron Ah, good! I see they've captured the Babes. Well done! Better tidy the place up a bit, don't want the alarm raised too soon. (*He picks up the bedsheet, takes it to the bed and starts to tidy up*)

Coke, Tizer and Nurse enter. She is still chasing them madly. They race across stage, making a tremendous din as they go. They exit the other side

The Baron presumably has not noticed them. He turns and comes down with a smug smile

I should think they've reached the woods by now. I've placed the pillows under the sheets, so anyone giving a casual glance would think the bed is occupied. (*He leans towards the audience in confidential mood*)
    Now please don't think too harsh of me,
    To do so would be folly,
    It isn't that I hate the Babes,
    It's just I need the lolly.

Music 16. SONG—BARON

The Baron exits after his song. Coke, Tizer and the Babes enter. The Robbers are pushing a perambulator in which sit Mark and Susan, who are now dressed in normal day clothes. They pause when they reach C

Susan Why are we being taken for a walk when it's time to go to bed?

Coke You're not being taken for a walk, you're being taken for a ride!

The Robbers laugh heartily

Mark I don't think that's funny. We were just in the middle of a lovely dream.

Susan Oh yes, a lovely dream about lovely dolls who all came to life and danced.

Coke Don't worry, that's nothing to the dance *we're* going to lead you.

The Robers go into fits of laughter again

Mark What were you doing in our bedroom in the first place?

Tizer Us? We're a couple of burg-u-lars.

Mark You're *not* a couple of burglars.

Tizer We are.

Susan You're not.

Tizer We are, honest!

Susan If you're a couple of burglars how can you be honest?

Coke We're professionals.

Susan You just said you were burglars.

Coke Professional burglars.

Act I, Scene 5

Susan You're not.
Coke We are.
Susan *I'll* tell you what *you* are.
Coke What, then?
Susan You're redundant.
Tizer (*to Coke*) What does she say?
Coke She reckons we're stagnant.
Susan (*raising her voice*) Both of you.
Coke Both of us are stagnant.
Tizer I thought I could smell something.
Mark Listen, you two fellers, do you know any riddles?
Tizer Do they have to be rude?
Mark No they don't have to be rude.
Tizer You start off and give us the right level, then.
Mark Er, what is it that's covered all over in fur and goes "mee-ow"?
Tizer I know—a cat.
Mark No, a kitten!

They all laugh

Susan What's most like a tabby cat looking out of a window?
Tizer Don't know.
Susan Another tabby cat looking in.

They all roar with laughter

Coke I know one! How is it that cats can see in the dark?
Mark / **Susan** Don't know. (*Speaking together*)
Coke Because they feed 'em on lights!

They all roll about

Mark Why is a man like a carpet?
Coke / **Tizer** Don't know. (*Speaking together*)
Mark Because, when he's down everybody walks on him.
Coke / **Tizer** Aaah! (*Speaking together*)
Susan Yes, and he is kept down by tacks (tax).

Coke (*aside to Tizer*) I believe they're a couple of communists. Well, come on—push up. Next stop Sherwood Forest.
Tizer (*who is letting Coke do all the work*) Oh, I'm so tired, I'll never make it.
Coke Come on, push up. We've got a job of work to do.
Tizer (*as they exit*) I'm so tired!

Coke and Tizer exit, pushing the Babes. Marion and Robin enter

Marion Don't make a noise, the Babes are sleeping.

They both look towards the bed and satisfy themselves it is occupied

Robin What I have to say is so confidential it won't wake a soul.

Music 17. PRODUCTION NUMBER

Robin begins to sing. This develops into a big Production Number. The Choristers enter, and any Principals as desired, to use as a build-up to the Finale of Act I. If stage facilities permit, this can evolve into a Transformation Scene

CURTAIN

ACT II

Scene 1

Sherwood Forest

The scene depicts a clearing in the forest. Trees and foliage are in the background and, if possible, a ground-row. There is a sloping bank in the centre of the clearing

As the CURTAIN *rises, Robin Hood's Men and all the Choristers are grouped around, some reclining, some standing, some sitting on logs, etc. They are laughing happily as the music goes into the opening number*

Music 18.

PRODUCTION NUMBER—CHORISTERS AND DANCERS

The music is bright and jolly. The Dancers enter and join in. It finishes on a tableau, then the dialogue takes over

Alan Yes, gentlemen, the forest is our home. This is where we live, where we are happy, where we belong.

Much Yes, Alan my boy, we are as much part of the forest as the little birds who nest in the trees.

Friar Maybe that's why our leader is called "Robin".

They all laugh, and go into a reprise of the Production Number

After a few bars, Robin and Marion enter amidst great excitement

Robin Listen everybody! I have distressing news!

They all rise to their feet

John What is it, Robin?

Robin The Babes have disappeared.

All What?

Robin Tell them, Marion.

Marion When I went to their nursery just now I discovered the bed was empty.

Will Don't worry, Marion, we'll find them!

All Aye-aye! We'll find them.
Robin Search the woods. Alan, you go that way, Much you go that way, Friar, up there; and John, take the road through the copse.

They all reply "aye-aye" as each takes a small group of people and exits in various directions. The music is reprised during the exits

Don't worry, Marion. My men know every inch of this forest, we'll soon have them under our care.
Marion They can't have got very far away.

Marion and Robin exit, talking as they go. Coke and Tizer, Mark and Susan enter from the opposite side. The Robbers are now sitting inside the perambulator and the Babes are pushing it. They struggle to the middle of the clearing before speaking

Coke (*to the Babes*) Come on, come on! You two are like a couple of elderly Senior Citizens.
Tizer Oh, I'm *so* tired!
Coke (*astonished*) You? Tired?
Tizer Yes.
Coke Riding all the way in the pram?
Tizer I don't think I've got enough strength to crawl out.
Coke (*crossly*) Come on, you kids, give poor Tizer a hand! Can't you see he's tired.
Tizer (*as they begin to help him out*) Careful now! Oh *do* be careful. I'm so delicate.
Coke Yes, he's got a floating kidney.
Tizer If it floats much higher it'll put my lights out.

The Babes get the Robbers to the ground, Coke takes a sword from the bottom of the pram and surveys the territory

Coke This looks a nice quiet spot to do it.
Susan What are you going to do?
Tizer We're going to do you in. You know, kill you. You won't feel a thing.
Susan (*brightly*) I don't want to be done in.
Mark You're very naughty boys, talking like that. Now stop it, otherwise we won't play with you.

Act II, Scene 1

Tizer Oh, that's done it.
Coke Who's done what?
Tizer He reckons if we kill 'em they won't play with us.
Coke I don't see why not. We're only doing our job.
Tizer (*to the Babes*) Yes, you see competition's very keen these days. If *we* don't do it your uncle will only go to Robin Hood.
Coke Yes, and he's just an amateur.
Mark What's Uncle got to do with it?
Coke Your uncle wants you out of the way. Then he can inherit your money and we get two hundred nickers.
Mark I don't believe it.
Coke Oh, it's true enough. We wouldn't tell a lie.
Susan It's not true! (*To Tizer*) Is it?
Tizer Cross my heart, and cut my throat. (*He suits the action to the word*)
Coke I wish you wouldn't use those expressions in front of the kids, just when we're going to kill 'em.
Tizer Oh well, they've got to learn to live with it, haven't they!
Mark I'm sorry, we must go home now.
Susan Otherwise Uncle won't take us to the pantomime.
Mark You two fellows ought to get a job as the clowns!

Mark and Susan laugh

Susan (*snuggling up to Tizer*) You're nice boys really. If you're very good we might invite you in for a cup of tea.
Tizer Anything to eat?
Mark Muffins! D'you like them?
Coke I like muffins but not crumpet.
Tizer I like crumpet!
Mark That's settled then.
Tizer (*to Coke*) D'you know something?
Coke What?
Tizer I'm not going to kill 'em.
Coke Don't be silly, there's two hundred nickers hanging on it.
Tizer I don't care how many nickers are hanging on it. They're nice kids, that little girl is proper dishy.
Coke *We've got to kill 'em!!*
Tizer Let's just give 'em a smack across the chops and take 'em home.

Coke No!
Tizer All right! I'll fight you for them.
Coke Right! (*He goes to the pram and takes out another sword*)

Choose your weapon!

Tizer (*taking the sword, which turns out to be very short, little more than dagger-length*) What's the idea?
Coke There's going to be a fight.
Tizer Who with?
Coke You and me.
Tizer I'll stop and see it.

Coke leaps about swishing his sword. Tizer keeps well out of his way—occasionally jabbing the air with his tiny weapon. Suddenly Tizer points upward

Look! Up there!
Coke (*turning round to look*) Where?
Tizer There! (*He stabs Coke in the rear*)

Coke wrests the sword from him and throws both into the pram. He then takes out two pistols, giving one to Tizer

Mark and Susan, becoming frightened, take each other by the hand and exit, unnoticed by the Robbers

Coke (*taking Tizer* C) We will now take eight steps, turn, and fire! Ready? Go!

Coke does an about-turn and takes eight large steps followed in step by Tizer, so that when Coke turns to fire they are face to face —noses almost touching

Fool! You should have gone the other way.
Tizer Can't. It's a one-way street!
Coke Give me that.

Coke flings the pistols back into the pram and brings out two pairs of boxing gloves. He invites Tizer to put one pair on saying, "Try 'em for size." He slips into his and commences some ostentatious shadow-boxing. Tizer looks on mesmerized, but eventually gets his gloves on and they do some sparring. They go into a clinch. The orchestra strikes up a waltz, played softly, and they waltz around

Act II, Scene 1   35

the stage together with Tizer getting more affectionate as it goes on. The music stops when Coke speaks

This is no good! Give me those! (*He throws the gloves back into the pram*) Trouble with you, you're a coward!

Tizer I'd rather be a coward than a corpse.

Coke then grasps Tizer's right hand and moulds it into a closed fist, placing it just under his chin and so that his right elbow is sticking out. He then raises Tizer's right leg in such a manner that his knee is immediately under his protruding right elbow. He then takes a few paces backward and takes a flying kick at Tizer's raised foot, kicking it upward, so that the continuity of movement—the knee hitting the elbow and the closed fist hitting his chin—knocks him out. He falls to the floor. Noises off help the effect. Coke kneels by his side. The Lights dim

You've killed me.
Coke No!
Tizer Yes!
Coke No!
Tizer Don't argue! I know if I'm killed or not!

A green light shines on Tizer

I'm dying.
Coke You're dying a good colour.
Tizer Gangrene's set in. I've gone mouldy.
Coke Tizer! I don't want you to die.
Tizer I don't want to die.
Coke And I don't *want* you to die.
Tizer Why don't you want me to die?
Coke I'd rather have you yester-die!
Tizer (*raising his head and looking downwards*) Oh dear!
Coke What's up, old chap!
Tizer There's a heck of a draught coming up here. Do you mind if I die over there?
Coke Not at all.

Tizer moves his position and flops down again face upward, but he gives his head a hefty whack as he lies back (noise off) and raises himself up to rub it. He then lies prone, lowering his head very gently

Tizer Do me a favour, Coke.
Coke Anything, Tizer, anything.
Tizer Tell all the people I owe money to . . .
Coke Yes?
Tizer That they are welcome to it.
Coke (*removing his hat*) Dead! Dead!

Two Men enter, carrying a stretcher. They are dressed in black and wear top hats draped with crepe

The Men walk slowly towards Tizer. Funeral music is heard from the orchestra. As Coke makes way, the Men lower the stretcher and place Tizer on it. It is a trick stretcher, so that when they lift it Tizer remains on the floor. They walk slowly towards the exit, Coke following with head bowed. Tizer gets up and follows Coke

Simultaneously Nurse enters, dressed as an angel, with wings and a halo. She hovers round the procession, ballet fashion, as everyone exits. Nurse is the last to go

The music stops and the Lights come up

Mark and Susan enter, still holding hands

Susan Oh, Mark! Where are we?
Mark I've no idea. I'm afraid we're lost.
Susan I'm *so* frightened!
Mark Yes, I am too—a bit.

The Lights begin to dim

Susan Look, it's getting dark.
Mark It must be very late.
Susan And I'm oh, so tired.
Mark Me too! Tell you what, there's a nice little mound up there.
Susan Where?
Mark Under the trees. See?

The Babes walk up to the mound

Act II, Scene 1

Let's rest here for a while. Come on, snuggle down. And Susan, don't worry. I'll look after you.

They put arms around each other and go to sleep

The Fairy enters

She tiptoes over to the Babes and waves her wand over them

Fairy Sleep tight, Babes,
    And rest assured I'll not be far away,
    Your bed is hard, the air is chill,
    But no cause for dismay.
I'll summon all the robins
    And birds of every hue,
To pluck the leaves from off the trees,
    And slowly cover you,
So you will have a blanket
    As warm as Fairy Snow,
And snugly you will dream your dreams,
    As through the night you go.

Music 19. BIRD BALLET

If the Fairy is a dancer she participates in the ballet. The smaller Dancers, dressed as birds, mime the covering of leaves. The Dance can then develop into a Point Ballet, or something on classical lines

The Dancers and Fairy exit after the ballet. Coke, Tizer and the Baron enter

Baron Have you done the deed?

Coke Yes, their bodies lie over there. (*He gives an indiscriminate wave of the hand*)

Baron Where?

Tizer (*giving an indiscriminate wave in the opposite direction*) Over there.

Baron You say "over there", and he says "over *there*". Which is it?

Tizer / **Coke** (*pointing in different directions*) Over there! (*Speaking together*)

The Baron goes stumping up to the mound and nearly falls over the sleeping Babes

Baron Ah! There they are!
Coke Eh?
Tizer What?
Baron There!
Tizer⎫
Coke⎭ Where? ⎱*(Speaking together)*⎰
Baron There! Poor little souls! I can't look, I can't look. (*He comes down, covering his eyes*) Wish to heaven I had never done it.

Coke and Tizer rush up and view the bodies. They cannot believe their eyes

Tizer Looks as though *someone's* done it.
Baron Well don't just stand there, get a shovel and bury them properly, in a grave. (*He bursts into tears as he makes for the exit*) I wish I'd never done it, I do. Wish I'd never done it.

The Baron exits, weeping copiously

Tizer That's a licker, ain't it?
Coke *Someone* must have done it.
Tizer P'raps it was the cold night air wot done 'em in.
Coke (*mimicking*) "Done 'em in?" What a way to talk in the presence of the deceased! You have no conscience.
Tizer Oh yes I have, I've seen it.
Coke You don't know the meaning of the word. Come here, I'll explain. Some years ago I was very poor.
Tizer Before the Welfare State made us all rich!
Coke Yes. I was walking about without a pair of shoes on my feet. Suddenly I came face to face with a shoe shop. Outside were three shelves of shoes, shoes marked ten pounds, shoes marked fifteen pounds, and shoes marked twenty pounds. I was about to steal a pair of those ten-pound shoes when some intangible force said, "You are stealing, put them back." That intangible force Tizer was my conscience. We all have a conscience, all of us!
Tizer (*after a pause*) You're quite right, Cokey. I did have one of those things that you had once.
Coke (*dramatically*) You, you had a conscience?
Tizer Yes. I too came to a shoe shop with shoes outside marked

Act II, Scene 1

like what you said. (*He becomes melodramatic*) I went up to that shoe shop, I put a pair of shoes marked ten pounds under my coat and as I walked away some tangerine force seemed to stop me. "It's no good," the voice said. "Put 'em back, it's no good."
Coke And you *didn't* steal that ten-pound pair of shoes?
Tizer No, I reached up and took a pair marked twenty-five quid!

Coke and Tizer exit

Lights dim to a deep blue

From all entrances come Robin Hood and His Men, also the Sheriff, Marion, Will and Village Girl

Each group carries a lighted lantern, and there is a reprise of the number which opened the scene played softly as background music. The groups cross-cross as they search for the Babes

Sheriff Search every nook and cranny. Leave no stone unturned.
Will It's so dark in the woods.
Sheriff Of course it's dark, it's night-time, what do you expect?
Robin I know every tree, every blade of grass in this forest. I'll search till the Babes are found.
Will Robin! Robin!
Robin Yes?
Will There's something here on this bank.
Marion (*by Will's side*) Bring more light.
Robin Where? Where?
Marion Under these leaves.

Everyone gathers round as the Babes are discovered. They are helped to their feet looking tired and a little dazed

Robin It's all right, children. It's us—see, Marion and your nurse, and all of us.
Marion (*snuggling them up*) You all right, children?
Mark (*surpressing a yawn*) Yes, thank you.
Susan A little tired, that's all.
Mark And cold.
Susan And hungry.

Everyone laughs

Marion Come on, we'll soon get you home.

There is a general exit, with the exception of the Sheriff and Nurse

Nurse Oh, Sheriff! Fancy me alone in the woods—with a man!
Sheriff Yes, well, good day, madam.
Nurse Now we're here I want to ask you a very personal question.
Sheriff Good grief! I believe she's going to propose!
Nurse All you have to do is say "Yes".
Sheriff She's after my money.
Nurse By the way, have you got any money.
Sheriff (*trying to get away*) I knew it!
Nurse (*pulling him back*) Just a pound will do.
Sheriff What is this, madam, blackmail?
Nurse No, it's a game. It's called Yes and No.
Sheriff Oh! What a relief.
Nurse It's very simple. If you say "Yes" you win, if you say "No" you lose.
Sheriff Very simple.
Nurse Hold your money up. Now, are you ready?
Sheriff Yes.
Nurse I didn't catch you that time, did I?
Sheriff Er—yes!
Nurse Splendid! You're doing fine, aren't you?
Sheriff Yes.
Nurse Oh, by the way, Sheriff—you haven't played this game before, have you?
Sheriff No! I swear it!
Nurse No, I thought not. You lose! (*She grabs the Sheriff's pound note*)

Music 20.

COMEDY DUET—SHERIFF AND NURSE

(*If possible the duet finishes on a burlesque dance*)

The Sheriff exits at the end of the number

Act II, Scene 1

Ah me, that's worn me out to a shadow. I think I'll have a little rest on this nice mossy bank. (*She sits on the mound*) Yes, nice and comfy. I'll see you in the morning.

The Lights dim to blue as she lies down to rest

Coke and Tizer enter. Coke is carrying a hefty garden spade and Tizer carries a small wooden spade used for making sand castles

Coke Come on, come on. Get cracking. We've got to get 'em buried before dawn.

They walk up to the mound and peer at the figure lying there

Tizer Is that 'em?

Coke picks up the Nurse's leg and waggles it about

Coke Yes. This one's the girl—I think!
Tizer She must have been reared on self-raising flour.
Coke I think she's suffering with elephantiasis. Drop your shovel and give me a hand, we'll bury 'em over there.

They make strenuous efforts lifting Nurse and get her a little way down. Then, breathing heavily, they put her down again

Tizer Are you thinking what I'm thinking?
Coke No! It *can't* be!

Nurse opens her eyes and gives a scream

Tizer *It is!*
Nurse Aaah! A man! A man!

Nurse chases them around the stage, it is very much a repeat of the scene in the Nursery, with the Robbers shouting "Help—Police —Murder, etc."

Coke and Tizer exit, pursued by Nurse

The Lights fade to a Black-out

Scene 2

On the Way to the Woods

As the Lights come up, Coke and Tizer enter. They are still being chased by Nurse. All three race across the stage and exit on the other side

Robin and Marion enter

Marion Oh, I'm so happy, and so grateful. The Babes are safe, thanks to you.
Robin I did no more than anyone else!
Marion You took us to the very spot, thanks to your knowledge of the forest.
Robin I'm glad you're happy.
Marion I am, extremely. Aren't you?
Robin It needs just one thing to complete my cup of happiness.
Marion Yes?
Robin (*very seriously*) That you, Maid Marion, accept my hand in marriage.
Marion I cannot accept the hand of one who's name I don't even know. Please, tell me about yourself. Who are you?
Robin I can't tell you that. I can't. I daren't!
Marion For heaven's sake, why not?
Robin It's—it's a secret.
Marion Your secret will be safe enough with me.
Robin If I tell you the truth you may refuse me.
Marion True love rides any obstacle—they say.
Robin Not this one.
Marion Then tell me again that you love me.

Music 21. DUET—ROBIN AND MARION

Robin and Marion exit at the end of the song. Coke and Tizer enter. They are exhausted, their steps falter, and they come to a halt

Coke I can't run any further.
Tizer Same here. I'm proper puffed!
Coke She'll have to catch us, that's all.

Act II, Scene 2

Nurse enters

Nurse Ah! There you are then. Got'cher, got'cher! (*She grabs the two Robbers, then realizes who they are*) Oh, for goodness sake—it's *you* couple of dopes. I thought you were a couple of men!
Coke (*aside*) And we thought you were the Babes!

The Robbers laugh

Nurse Well, I can't waste my time talking to you crummy lot, I've got to get changed for the ball tonight.
Coke What ball?
Nurse The Baron's giving a ball as a welcome-present to the two Babes.

The Robbers go into fits of laughter

Coke (*aside to Tizer*) She doesn't know they've snuffed it.
Tizer Don't tell her.
Nurse (*shouting over them*) And *I've* been invited.
Tizer *We're* going to the Baronial Hall tonight, too.
Coke To cream the kitty!
Tizer Money on the table. Nickers strewn everywhere!
Nurse What are you talking about?
Coke It's a little debt the Baron owes us.
Tizer For services rendered.
Nurse Well, if you're coming to the ball you'll have to learn a song.
Tizer I'd like to learn a song.
Nurse All right, we'll *all* learn a song.

Music 22.

CHORUS SONG—NURSE, COKE AND TIZER

(*This is the usual chorus with audience participation, in which children from the auditorium can be invited to join in*)

Scene 3

The Baronial Hall

It is beautiful and ostentatious, with a maximum of colour. There is a rostrum running at the back with a large staircase leading from it in the centre, and this is framed by two huge pillars

As the Curtain *rises, the Baron's guests are gavorting around in gorgeous attire*

Music 23. STATELY NUMBER

(This should be in keeping with the situation and can finish with a rather pompous dance)

During the number, or immediately after, the Principals come down the staircase in the following order: Will Scarlet, Coke and Tizer, Sheriff, Marion, Nurse. They walk majestically and join various groups in conversation

The music stops abruptly as the Baron enters and makes a dramatic gesture at the top of the staircase

Everyone looks at him

Baron Your attention, everybody! (*After a pause*) I have some very grave news to impart. A most dreadful thing has happened. The Babes—the Babes are dead!
All Dead?
Baron Killed, and buried in Sherwood Forest.

Robin Hood enters, followed by Mark and Susan

Robin No Baron! The Babes are here! Alive and well!
Baron What? It can't be! My darlings . . . (*He goes forward to embrace the children*)

The Babes turn away from the Baron and run to Maid Marion

(*Turning on Coke and Tizer*) You told me they were dead!
Robin Yes, and it was you, Baron, who ordered their death.
Coke Correct! The Baron offered us two hundred pieces of gold to kill the babes, so that he could inherit their fortune.

Act II, Scene 3   45

There is a gasp from the crowd

Baron You cannot take the word of a robber.
Sheriff They have turned King's Evidence.
Robin You are the real robber, Baron. And a murderer, too!
Baron I know that voice! Robin Hood! That man is Robin Hood! Arrest him.

There is reaction from the crowd, and Marion goes up to Robin

Marion So that's who you are, Robin Hood!

Robin makes to reply, but she turns on her heel

Baron (*shouting*) Arrest that man. He is Robin Hood!

There is a half-hearted movement towards Robin

Friar Robin Hood is a hero.
Much But for his knowledge of the woods the babes would have perished.
John Release him!
Alan Three cheers for Robin Hood.

They all cheer

Nurse (*coming forward*) And arrest the real villain—the wicked Uncle!

At a sign from the Sheriff they move away from Robin Hood and surround the Baron

Susan Oh please, *please*! It's Christmas time. Can't we forgive and forget.

Susan runs to the Baron, who falls on his knees and embraces her

Mark I'm sure Uncle didn't really mean to harm us.

Mark runs to the Baron and joins in the embrace. There is an awkward pause

Baron If only you'll forgive me I'll be the best wicked uncle that ever was.
Robin (*turning to Marion*) And if only *you* will forgive *me* I'll be the best wicked husband that ever was!

Sheriff (*hesitating*) Well, as they say, "out of the mouths of babes..."

Nurse (*mincing up to the Sheriff*) And if only I can bring myself to forgive *you* I'll be the prettiest bride that ever was at your wedding.

Sheriff Well, good night, everybody.

The Sheriff exits

Marion (*to Robin*) Of course I forgive you—with all my heart.

Baron And the wedding reception shall be held here, in the Baronial Hall, at my expense.

Robin You mean "at the Babes' expense", don't you?

Everyone laughs

Music 24. BRIGHT PRODUCTION NUMBER

At the end of the number, all exit

Music 25. DANCERS' SPECIALITY

Music 26. MARCH DOWN

The whole Company march down the staircase in the following order:

> *Chorus Ladies and Gentleman*
> *Speciality Dancers*
> *Much-the-Miller, Little John, Alan-a-Dale, Friar Tuck*
> *Will Scarlet, Village Girl*
> *Sheriff*
> *Baron*
> *Nurse Maxidrawers*
> *Coke, Tizer*
> *Mark, Susan*
> *Robin Hood, Maid Marion*

The music fades under the following dialogue

Robin And so we say Farewell,
       For that's our story told,

Act II, Scene 3

Marion	A tale that isn't new,
	And yet it's never old.
Sheriff	We've proved that crime just doesn't pay,
	You saw the fate of Unky's,
Nurse	He now says that he's sorry, but
	He doesn't give a monkey's!
Coke	We never had our money,
	It does seem rather hard,
Baron	But I have got no money,
Tizer	Well, use your Access Card!
Fairy	There's only one thing left to say,
	A message understood, It's
All	Good night from every one of us,
Babes	And Good Luck—From the Babes in the Wood!

Music 27. FINALE CHORUS

(*This may, if desired, be a repeat chorus of one of the numbers used in the production*)

CURTAIN

FURNITURE AND PROPERTY LIST

ACT I

Scene 1

On stage: Bell on **Baron's** front door
Flowers and greenery

Off stage: Notice of Reward and drawing pin (**Sheriff**)
Large visiting card (**Tizer**)
Luggage (**Mark, Susan**)
Wand (**Fairy**)
Larger Notice of Reward (**Sheriff**)

Scene 3

On stage: Teacher's desk. *On it:* cane
Blackboard
Long forms for pupils

Off stage: Handbell (**Teacher/Nurse**)
Empty beer bottle with rose in it (**Baron**)
Large unblown balloon (**Tizer**)

Scene 5

On stage: Double bed and bedding, nightgown under pillow. *Under it:* hatbox containing mob-cap
Small table

Off stage: Lighted candle (**Nurse**)
Large tool bag with tools (**Tizer**)
Large perambulator (**Tizer, Coke**)

ACT II

Scene 1

On stage: Trees, foliage
Sloping bank
Logs

Off stage: 2 swords set in bottom of pram, one very short **(Coke, Tizer)**
2 pistols set in bottom of pram **(Coke, Tizer)**
2 pairs of boxing gloves set in bottom of pram **(Coke, Tizer)**
Trick stretcher **(Funeral Men)**
Wings, halo **(Nurse)**
Lanterns **(Search Parties)**
Garden spade **(Coke)**
Small wooden seaside spade **(Tizer)**

LIGHTING PLOT

Note: the following cues occur in the action of the story. Further cues, such as follow spots during the songs, may of course be added as facilities allow
Property fittings required: nil
Various simple exterior and interior scenes

ACT I

To open: Bright overall lighting
Cue 1	At end of Scene 1	(Page 14)
	Cross-fade to front-cloth lighting	
Cue 2	At the end of Scene 2	(Page 16)
	Cross-fade to overall interior lighting—schoolroom	
Cue 3	At the end of Scene 3	(Page 22)
	Cross-fade to **Babes**, *then to front-cloth lighting*	
Cue 4	At the end of Scene 4	(Page 24)
	Cross-fade to interior lighting, evening, nursery	
Cue 5	**Babes** snuggle down to sleep	(Page 25)
	General dim of all lighting, spot on **Fairy**: *bring up special lighting for Dance, revert to dim lighting on general exit*	
Cue 6	**Nurse** blows out candle	(Page 26)
	Further dim of lighting by bed	
Cue 7	**Baron** enters	(Page 27)
	Bring up lighting slightly, except on bed	
Cue 8	**Robin:** "... it won't wake a soul."	(Page 30)
	Gradually bring up special lighting for Act I finale	

ACT II

To open: Overall lighting, for forest scene
Cue 9	**Tizer** falls to ground	(Page 35)
	Lights dim	
Cue 10	**Tizer:** "I know if I'm killed or not!"	(Page 35)
	Bring up green spot on **Tizer**	

Cue 11	As **Tizer** walks off *Fade spot, return lighting to full*	(Page 36)
Cue 12	**Mark**: "Yes, I am too—a bit." *Dim general lighting, retain spot on mound*	(Page 36)
Cue 13	**Fairy**: "As through the night you go." *Cross-fade to special Bird Ballet lighting—revert to former lighting as Ballet ends*	(Page 37)
Cue 14	**Coke** and **Tizer** exit *Dim all lighting to deep blue*	(Page 39)
Cue 15	**Nurse**: "You lose." *Cross-fade to special lighting for duet. At finish, revert to deep blue*	(Page 40)
Cue 16	**Coke, Tizer** and **Nurse** exit *Fade to Black-out, then up to front-cloth lighting*	(Page 41)
Cue 17	At end of Scene 2 *Bring up all lighting to full*	(Page 43)

EFFECTS PLOT

ACT I

No cues

ACT II

Cue 1	**Tizer** falls on ground *Noise of 'Kicking gag'*	(Page 35)
Cue 2	**Tizer** lies back, cracking head on ground *Exaggerated bang, off*	(Page 35)

www.ingramcontent.com/pod-product-compliance
Ingram Content Group UK Ltd.
Pitfield, Milton Keynes, MK11 3LW, UK
UKHW021847210426
5322IPUK00022B/526